FE

and

YOUR OFFICE

Creativity in this project is the result of warm, inspirational love from my three lovely little grand-daughters, Anjuli, Ella and Mia

FENG SHUI
and
YOUR OFFICE

Aroon Ajmera

Illustrated by Gordon Redrup

FENG SHUI DESIGNS

© Aroon Ajmera 2002
Illustrations © Gordon Redrup

Published in 2002 by Feng Shui Designs
Sarika, 57 Armitage Rd, London NW11 8QT

Distributed by Gazelle Book Services Limited, Falcon House
Queen Square Lancaster, England LA1 1RN

British Library Cataloguing in Publication Data
A catalogue record for this book is available from the British Library

ISBN 0-9542462-0-9

Typeset by Amolibros, Watchet, Somerset
This book production has been managed by Amolibros
Printed and bound by T J International Ltd, Padstow, Cornwall, UK

ABOUT THE AUTHOR

Born in India, Aroon graduated from New York University in 1961 with a Master's Degree in Business Administration. He has lived in London, UK since 1967. In spite of being a busy banker for twenty-three years, he began his pursuit of Intuitive® Feng Shui at the age of fifty-six under one of the world's leading Feng Shui consultants and teachers, William Spear.

This new field has been the sole focus of his career since 1996, leading him to set up Feng Shui Designs Ltd, now a well-established Feng Shui consultancy firm with an ever-expanding international client base.

He also pioneered the creation of the first Feng Shui photographic online Gallery. In addition to transforming his clients' lives through his consultations, Aroon also teaches Feng Shui and is the author of the best-selling book, *Feng Shui and Your Home*.

He can be contacted at:

Feng Shui Designs Ltd, *Sarika, 57 Armitage Road,*
London NW11 8QT
Tel/fax: +44 (0) 20 8455 1158
E-mail: AAjmera999@aol.com
Web site: www.fengshuidesigns.co.uk
Photo Gallery: www.photobox.co.uk/fengshuidesigns

CONTENTS

Part Two

FOREWORD

Although it is as old as the hills, the popularity for Feng Shui in the West only really started in the early 1990s. More than a passing fad, it is definitely here to stay as interest in this fascinating subject continues to grow. Aroon Ajmera was among those who were on that first wave of interest, the pioneers who were hungry for this new knowledge. I remember Aroon attending a talk I gave at an interior design exhibition in London. It really fired up his imagination and started him out on a long journey studying this ancient wisdom. Since then his new career has seen him teach all over the world and make a difference to the lives of many people. He has packed a lot of great information into this simple list of tips which is no small achievement.

The principles of Feng Shui are as relevant in the workplace as they are in the home and with many people spending a large proportion of their time there, it is extremely important to make sure that their office environment is balanced. This book will give you an easy and useful starting point for creating a more harmonious and less stressful office.

Enjoy.

Gina Lazenby
July 2002
Co-founder of the Feng Shui Society and author of
The Healthy Home, Feng Shui House Book and
Simple Feng Shui

INTRODUCTION

I have written this little book to give you some tips for creating a supportive and harmonious environment in your office.

The constantly changing invisible energy forces in an office can have a dramatic impact not only on the physical, emotional and spiritual wellbeing of its employees but also the health of the business. Offices already use the services of interior designers to enhance the comfort and aesthetics of the working environment.

By incorporating the Feng Shui principles in the layout of an office, staff morale, creativity and team spirit can be positively influenced. This in turn reduces absenteeism and staff turnover. Inappropriate conflict and internal competition between employees can also be diluted.

When you pay attention to how and where people sit, and the colours, materials and amount of natural light in an environment, their efficiency will soar, making a significant contribution to the success and the profitability of a business.

This book weaves the principles of Feng Shui into the interior design of your office and ultimately helps you create a stress-free working environment.

Read it, enjoy it and transform your business into one that is healthy, creative, stable and successful.

Aroon Ajmera
July 2002

PART ONE

PART ONE

*"We shape our buildings, thereafter
they shape us."*

Winston Churchill

WHAT IS FENG SHUI?

The direct translation of Feng Shui (pronounced Fung Schway) is "Wind and Water", the two elements of nature that shape our very existence. Feng Shui can be defined as the practice of analysing and influencing the interaction of people, buildings and the environment, which ultimately leads to happier and more successful lives.

Originating in ancient China, its basis is the understanding of a vital energy force called "Ch'i". It has been used in the Orient for over 3,000 years and is a body of knowledge, which links our inner self to our outer environment.

4

Feng Shui enables us to create environments suitable for their intended activity by identifying the imbalances and adjusting them to enhance the quality of our lives.

CH'I

T he underlying principle of Feng Shui is Ch'i. Ch'i is simply the energy that surrounds us in all forms of life. Ch'i can be of the earth, the atmosphere or of people. The quality of Ch'i is expressed through form, shape, colour, sound and the feelings that it generates.

The Ch'i of the earth can be negative or positive. Negative earth energies can have detrimental effects on the immune system and the human psyche. Detection of their paths and manipulation can enhance our emotional stability and prevent long-term illnesses.

The paths of Ch'i flowing within the body are called meridians and the manipulation of Ch'i within these meridians forms the basis of acupuncture, acupressure and shiatsu.

WHAT ENERGIES
ARE TO BE ALIGNED?

There are three different sources of Ch'i:

1 Heaven's energy—or astrological energy of our time—provides us with a source of guidance.

2 Our own energy—'wind and water' (in the form of our breath and blood) inside our body.

3 Earth's energy—or the energy of our environment.

8

We can influence our own energy with a proper diet, discipline and meditation for our body, mind and spirit. The energy of our environment can be altered through Feng Shui tools such as colours, materials and shapes.

YIN AND YANG

YIN AND YANG

These are the two cosmic forces of energy which are opposite, yet complementary. There is no balance in the universe without both of them. The forces of heaven are Yang and the forces of earth are Yin.

Yang is: light, dry, loud, hard, full, hot, active, sun, fire, male, summer, day, and contracting, gathering, durable, horizontal, thicker and smaller.

Yin is: dark, wet, quiet, soft, empty, cold, passive, moon, water, female, winter, night, expanding, dispersing, delicate, vertical, thinner and bigger.

For positive, auspicious Feng Shui there must be balance and harmony between Yin and Yang.

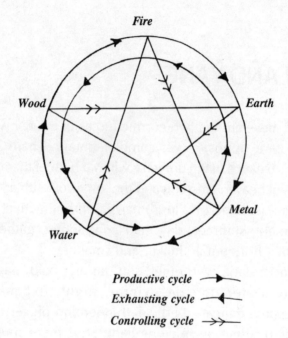

THE FIVE ELEMENTS

THE FIVE ELEMENTS

Much of Feng Shui theory is based on understanding how these elements (earth, metal, water, wood and fire) interact in the physical environment, resulting in either harmony or imbalance.

The elements are involved in three kinds of cyclical relationships—the productive, the exhaustive and the controlling cycle.

The productive cycle runs clockwise. The exhaustive cycle runs anti-clockwise. The arrows within the diagram represent the controlling cycle.

13

In interior decor, the elements are represented by colours, shapes and materials. When an environment needs balancing, one way to solve the imbalance is to add or subtract the colour, shape or material that each element expresses.

Element	Colour	Shapes	Material
FIRE	red	pointed or triangular shapes pyramids	plastic diamonds
EARTH	yellow brown	squares, flat shapes	ceramics, clay, plaster, china, bricks, soft stone
METAL	white, gold, silver	spheres, circles, domes, arches, ovals, round shapes	stainless steel, brass, copper, bronze, iron, silver, gold, marble
WATER	black, blue	wavy lines, irregular shapes	glass
WOOD	green, dark green	rectangles, tall, vertical shapes	wood and paper

GEOPATHIC STRESS

G eopathic Stress" means disease derived from the earth through the negative energies rising up the buildings. Occupants can lose their physical strength, energy, emotional stability and happiness. It can also cause serious long-term illnesses.

Being in close proximity of electromagnetic radiation of power transmission lines, radios, computers, mobile phones, printers or lamps, increases the effects of "Geopathic Stress". Anything that disturbs the natural magnetic field of the earth (metal furniture frames, beams, radiators and plumbing, etc.) can have an adverse effect on our well-being.

WHAT DOES EACH FENG SHUI CURE DO?

★ Mirrors give us an increased sense of space and deflect negativity.
★ Wind chimes prevent negativity and moderate energy flow.
★ Lights fill any missing areas and lift the energy of the space.
★ Flowers create happy Ch'i.
★ Plants represent growth and shield you against poison arrows from sharp corners.
★ Water fountains/ponds enhance prosperity.

★ Paintings/sculptures uplift our Ch'i and can be used as symbols of protection.
★ Crystals energise areas with vibrant rainbow colours.
★ Colours, used appropriately, lift energy levels.

SCHOOLS OF FENG SHUI

There are three principal schools of Feng Shui:

★ Form School
★ Traditional Chinese Compass School
★ Black Hat Sect School

Although the basic principles remain the same, each one has a slightly different approach to the subject.

***

The Form School focuses on the contours of landscapes, in particular their shape, size and the relationship between the physical formations and a dwelling. The directions are symbolised by four celestial animals. The East relates to the Green Dragon, the West to the White Tiger, the South to the Red Phoenix and the North to the Black Tortoise. The most auspicious locations for premises are derived by surveying the landscape.

***

The Traditional Chinese Compass School uses magnetic directions to identify the flow of Ch'i coming from different directions, by dividing the space into eight areas of life. South represents Fame, North represents Career, East for Elders or Past, West for Children or Future, Southeast refers to Prosperity, Southwest to Relationships, Northwest to Mentors or

Helpful friends and Northeast to Knowledge or Wisdom.

$$***$$

The Black Hat Sect School is the most recent one where each house or office or room is judged from the position of the main door. The Bagua template is used and the main door is aligned to Career, Knowledge or the Helpful Friends sector to determine the location of the other sectors.

This book uses this simplified method to enable the easy implementation of recommendations for your office.

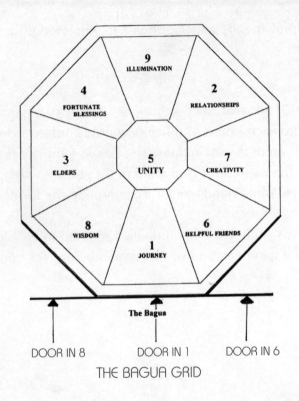

THE BAGUA GRID

HOW TO USE THE BAGUA GRID

Place the Bagua on top of the floor plan of your office in such a way that the front door of your office lines up with segments 8, 1 or 6 along the thick base line. You will then be able to identify the spaces in your office corresponding to all the areas of your life.

Remember that you can also place the Bagua over the plan of each room (such as a private office) in the same way.

DEFINITIONS

Area	Name	Relates to your
1	Journey	Progression
2	Relationships	Clients and Colleagues
3	Elders	Bosses or Advisers
4	Fortunate Blessings	Wealth/Prosperity
5	Unity	Health of the Enterprise

Area	Name	Relates to your
6	Helpful Friends	Guidance/Source of inspiration
7	Creativity	New Projects/Future
8	Wisdom	Knowledge/Contemplation
9	Illumination	Fame/Recognition

PART TWO

THE BUILDING

THE BUILDING

GOOD LOCATION

Look out for a quality environment for your office. Other successful businesses, plenty of trees, flowing water embracing the front of the building, coupled with open space and tall buildings behind, all contribute to good Feng Shui for your office.

AVOID POISON ARROWS

Ensure that your office building is not located at a street's dead end or at a T-junction. The flow of negative energy can destroy the space and bring misfortune. If this cannot be avoided, safeguard the space by creating a wall or planting shrubs or hedges. As a last resort, place a small mirror above the door or in a window facing the street to deflect the negative energy.

DO NOT BE A SITTING TARGET

Ensure that tall telephone poles, streetlights, or sharp edges of nearby buildings are not facing your front door. Deflect their poison arrows by placing a Bagua shaped mirror either on the front door or in the window as appropriate.

SHAPE MATTERS

The most auspicious configurations for a building are rectangular, square or gently curving and the latter is the most harmonious of the three. A modular shape is more harmonious than a sharp-edged one. Your building should not look hostile in relation to others in the neighbourhood as this may cause problems with harmonious relationships.

ENERGY MUST BE CONTAINED

Buildings with clear glass walls on all sides are undesirable, as the ch'i will escape. Having at least two adjoining solid walls in the design would conserve the ch'i. Reflective glass-tiled wall buildings are also less desirable, as the ch'i will be deflected away.

AVOID A CASCADING SHAPE

Buildings with narrowing shape on upper floors and cascading steps in its external design are also undesirable, as the occupants of such buildings are likely to find it difficult to conserve their prosperity. The energy slides down rapidly.

BE IN HARMONY WITH NATURE

A landscaped garden with a water feature facing the front entrance brings in auspicious Ch'i to the premises. Tortoises and fish in a pond depict success; rockeries represent stability whilst streams and plants symbolise wealth and growth.

DOORWAY AND ENTRANCE SIZE

According to Feng Shui, the most important part of any building is its main door, which in a sense is its mouth. A large entrance to your office is desirable as it brings in positive vibrations to your premises. Revolving doorways are considered good as they constantly renew the flow of energy.

THE RECEPTION

THE RECEPTION

FIRST IMPRESSIONS

You never get a second chance to make a first impression. Ensure that your reception is spacious, welcoming, has a good combination of colours, textures, surfaces in terms of Yin and Yang, good lighting and adequate room for the energy to flow.

CREATE A PARADISE

Visitors should feel the harmony in the atmosphere. Create a welcoming scenario with plants, water features such as fish tanks and fountains, soft colours and eye-catching artwork.

PROJECT A HEALTHY SET-UP

Ensure the reception desk is uncluttered. The environment moulds the morale of the receptionist and gives your visitors a message about the overall health of your business.

MAKE THE JOURNEY EVEN MORE PLEASANT

Lifts and stairways to other parts of the building should be conveniently located, spacious and tidy. Remember, at this stage, your guests have started forming an impression of your organisation and its image.

CLUTTER...

CLUTTER

GIVE A LIFT TO YOUR ENERGY

When you clear clutter in your office, on your desk, in filing cabinets or your computer, you pave the way for new things and new projects, giving a lift to your creativity and energy.

KEEP THE ENERGY FLOWING

Corridors in your office linking private offices and open-plan areas are like arteries of energy, providing nourishment to the entire office space. Keep them clutter-free for an overall healthy atmosphere.

CLEAR YOUR DESK

Clutter is the enemy of good Feng Shui. Keep your desk clear and let the energy flow freely around you. Keep files off the floor. Discard what you really don't need.

AVOID SPAGHETTI SCENARIO

Tangled or exposed electrical and computer cables represent clutter, thereby enhancing the risk of physical accidents and fire. Keeping them concealed dramatically reduces subconscious stress levels.

AVOID A CRASH

Clutter within a computer such as undeleted old e-mails and programs in your system that you never use, slow down the pace of your system and adversely affect your productivity. Just like your filing cabinets and desk, your computer needs to be de-cluttered at regular intervals.

MAKE A CLEAN POLICY

Clutter on your windowsills and dirty windows give you a murky view of the outer world. Keep the energy fresh and alive by keeping windows clean, regular vacuuming and dusting.

REPAIR OR REPLACE BROKEN GADGETS

Anything that isn't working represents clutter and contributes to increased stress levels. Light bulbs, clocks, wall sockets, taps, chairs or even air-conditioners should be repaired or replaced at once.

DO NOT AMPLIFY YOUR PROBLEMS

Do not place cures and enhancements such as crystals, plants and water features before clearing the clutter. Otherwise you may double your problems rather than resolve them.

SUPPORTIVE ENVIRONMENT

SUPPORTIVE ENVIRONMENT

PENDING MATTERS SLOW YOU DOWN

Watch out for big piles of "in" tray. The higher the stack, the more you will feel overwhelmed. Mountains of paperwork make you feel defeated before you have even started. A clear desk means a clear mind, better creativity and more job satisfaction.

PEACE ENHANCES PRODUCTIVITY

Noise pollution from computers, printers, copiers, traffic, telephones and air-conditioning systems are the most disruptive factors in offices. Where possible, try to isolate noisy equipment from working areas.

LIGHTING LIFTS YOUR CH'I

Lighting must be good. Research shows that people are much more motivated and healthier if they sit near windows. Dark corners are lifeless areas.

FEEL SAFE

Don't hang any plants or have lights suspended directly above your head. Desk lamps are OK. Office lighting is often another energy-draining source and must be adjusted as required for the comfort of the staff's eyesight. Light colour schemes create a nurturing environment.

CREATE A COMFORT ZONE

If the atmosphere is too cold, too hot or too dry, then rectify the situation by using humidifiers, lush plants and appropriate images containing cooling shades of blue or warming shades of red.

CLEAN AIR IS VITAL

Toxic chemicals from furniture create air pollution and computers generate electromagnetic fields. Deal with these by regular cleaning and ventilation. Placing plants and raw crystals help absorb negative vibrations and cleanse the environment.

IDENTIFY NEGATIVE EARTH ENERGY

Dowsing can help detect areas that contain Geopathic Stress and negative earth energies. Relocating the desks or clearing the space with the help of an expert can prevent poor health, low performance and the inexplicable irritability of staff.

CHOICE OF COLOURS

Colours affect your energy levels although the choice is a subjective matter. Pale colours for walls are often recommended as strong colours have greater influence on your emotions and the effect filters through to the quality of your work.

COLOUR CAN BE A BALANCING TOOL

Cream generates warmth and helps in reception areas. Blue calms the nerves and lowers noise in areas with too much activity. Yellow promotes creativity, green enhances judgement and white is suitable for creating a feeling of spaciousness and purity.

ENSURE A VISUAL FLOW

The transition from the colour of the carpet to the wall colour must be soothing to the eye and complementary. This promotes harmony in the environment.

FLOOR-COVERING SIGNIFICANCE

Wooden floors create rising energy and stimulate lively conversations whereas natural wool carpets make you feel calmer and grounded. The first option will therefore be more suitable for a place like a staff canteen and the latter would be ideal for offices and meeting rooms.

BLOCK EXCESSIVE SUNLIGHT

Excessive sunlight through windows creates very active energy with glaring and hot sunrays. Using heavy drape curtains or suitable roller blinds are preferable to using conventional blinds. Sharp blades like edges of blinds create poison arrows.

FURNITURE DESIGN AND CONFIGURATION

FURNITURE DESIGN
AND CONFIGURATION

DESK SHAPE, SURFACE AND COLOUR

Desk shapes and surfaces can have a significant impact on your energy levels. Round-edged desks are generally preferable, as they tend to support creativity. However, square furniture is better for money and management. Natural and light wood colours are preferable to contrast black or white colours. Non-reflective surfaces are better than highly polished or glass surfaces.

THE THRONE

Chairs should ideally have a stable five-spoke base, adjustable height, tilt mechanism for the seat and supportive armrests as our breathing and digestion depends on the positioning of our arms.

VANTAGE POINT

Make sure your desk is diagonally facing the door, so that you are in control of the room and you can see who is coming in. If your back is to the entrance you will subconsciously feel uneasy and this will drain your energy. Place a small mirror on your desk to rectify this problem.

SIT LIKE A KING

Sit with a solid wall behind you rather than an open space. This will enhance your feeling of being supported. If you have a window or a walkway behind you, reinforce your defences with a bookcase or, at the very least, a plant.

BE THE FOCAL POINT

Avoid putting pictures and art above your head. Don't let the attention of your visitors be distracted from you.

DON'T BE SWEPT AWAY

Avoid sitting in the line of energy, i.e. facing a door, a large window or someone else within two metres of you. This can disrupt harmony. Place plants or a small barrier to shield yourself if the desk arrangement cannot be changed.

TAKE THE WEIGHT OFF YOUR HEAD...

Avoid sitting under large beams, overhead shelves or cupboards. Sitting under suppressed energy fields will stifle your growth or promotion prospects.

AVOID BEING TARGETED

Avoid having the edges of walls or the sharp corners of large furniture like filing cabinets and bookshelves pointing directly at you. These create poison arrows or cutting Ch'i, which is harmful for your well-being. Placing leafy plants in front of the edges helps neutralise the negative effects.

BALANCE THE ENERGIES

Open-plan offices already have Yang (active) energy. Maintain the balance by avoiding the use of bright colours.

ISOLATION WITHOUT PRIVACY

Workstations such as cubicles in an open-plan office resemble a maze and are not productive as they seem to lower the staff morale.

SOME PRECAUTIONS

In a workstation layout, ensure that a screen is supporting your back and the entrance to your area is within your full view.

STRIKE A BALANCE

Open-plan offices with workstations need to incorporate a level of privacy together with ease of communication with other colleagues. Wave-shaped desk-dividing screens are ideal for creating this balance.

EQUIPMENT

EQUIPMENT (COMPUTERS, TELEPHONES AND MOBILE PHONES)

LIBRARY LEVEL PEACE

Photocopiers, fax machines, computers and printers create excessive noise pollution. Try to isolate these in a space away from working areas.

RAISE THE COMFORT LEVEL

Prevent the energy drain by raising the comfort level. Be it an anti-glare screen, a radiation filter for eyestrain, a more comfortable keyboard or a nicely shaped mouse. Have it.

KEEP A SAFE DISTANCE

Sit at least three feet away from the back of a computer to avoid the ill effects of electromagnetic fields. Place a plant near the computer to create humidity in the environment and a raw crystal such as an amethyst to absorb any harmful negativity in the area.

COMMUNICATION PORT

Place the telephone in the far right corner of your desk (the relationship area) to get the best out of any interaction with colleagues and clients.

BE TIDY—LOOK SMART

Telephone cords and computer cables should be well concealed and should not therefore run across your desk.

AVOID YOGA POSITIONS

Cradling the phone between your neck and shoulder can block your 'Ch'i' and accelerate a feeling of fatigue.

HEALTH HAZARD

Mobile phones can expose you to excess electromagnetic radiation and should be used as little as possible.

IMAGES, ARTWORK & PLANTS

IMAGES, ARTWORK AND PLANTS

VISUAL VIBRATIONAL WORLD

Symbology is important in Feng Shui. Check to see what negative and positive messages are being given out by the choice of posters and art around you. Are they dull, flat and limiting landscapes? Stark, aggressive images? Abstract and confusing lines without clarity?

AVOID NEGATIVE VIBRATIONS

Negative images include battle scenes, sinking ships, swords, daggers, missiles, sunsets, waterfalls or anything dead, e.g. plants, fishes, animals or people. Positive images include sunrises, birds in flight, flowers, parks, gardens and landscapes. Negative images drain our energy whereas positive ones lift our spirits.

SCULPTURES ADD STABILITY

Sculptures enhance stability and add grace to the environment. Ensure that the sculptures selected are in proportion to the space they are displayed in and that they project positive vibrations.

CREATE A FOCAL POINT

First impressions are important—make sure your visitors see something like a plant or a work of art, something on which to focus their energy when they enter a room. It will help them to feel more comfortable and relaxed.

LOGO & STATIONERY DESIGN PRINCIPLES

LOGO AND STATIONERY
DESIGN PRINCIPLES

MESSAGE FROM A LOGO

A logo gives out a message about a business and sometimes its products too. It should therefore be identifiable, attractive and appropriate and convey the stability of the company by a shape that is supportive and solid.

IMAGE CREATION

Your logo also creates a corporate identity. It is the visual representation of the company and what it stands for. It should symbolise power, authority and the vitality of your enterprise.

EVALUATE

Is your logo merely a design at environmental level or does it project anything about your company such as its skills, its values, its identity and its spirit? You can check this with regard to the needs and the vision of the company.

DESIGN RULES

Consider the choice of name, purpose of logo and its location on business cards and stationery.

TIME LINES

Incorporate time lines. The future is to the right and up; past is to the left and down. If the design incorporates layers, the future is in front and the past is behind.

SIMPLICITY IS THE BEST POLICY

Keep the text, image and use of colours simple and in proportion to the size and the shape of the logo.

SHAPE SIGNIFICANCE

An oval shape like a womb is caring. A circular shape signifies global presence. A square box indicates stability. A sound foundation is projected by a solid base line.

DESIGN TIPS

A good design incorporates visual balance, avoids downward arrows depicting decline, and does not use a cross in the central part as this signifies unresolved problems.

VISUAL FLOW

Maintain a connection between the name, address, your name and the logo on a business card. The simplicity of less text and a clutter-free layout conveys more and creates a lasting impact.

STAFF PLACEMENT GUIDE & THE BAGUA

PLACEMENT GUIDE FOR STAFF & THE BAGUA

Area No 1—Journey

Journey represents your career path and progression. The RECEPTION for your office may be located in this space as it is the entrance to your organisation.

Area No 2—Relationships

The Relationships area is associated with your receptivity, dealings with your staff and colleagues. The PERSONNEL department could be allocated to this space.

Area No 3—Elders

The Elders area relates to your foundation, roots and ancestors and in a business environment your ultimate boss. Ideally, your CHAIRMAN'S OFFICE could be here.

Area No 4—Fortunate Blessings

The Fortunate Blessings area generates the auspicious omens of the material world. The FINANCIAL CONTROLLER or THE ACCOUNTS department may be located here.

Area No 5—Unity

Unity is the central area of your organisation and should be kept uncluttered. If you have to use this space, have an INTERNAL MEETING room here.

Area No 6—Helpful Friends

The Helpful Friends area relates to generosity in terms of time, money and friends. Your MANAGING DIREC-TOR'S office may be located here.

Area No 7—Creativity

Creativity corresponds to new ideas, projects or your future. A BOARDROOM or a MEETING ROOM would be most suitable in this space.

Area No 8—Wisdom

The Wisdom area represents meditation and contemplation. The RESEARCH and DEVELOPMENT department could be allocated to this space.

Area No 9—Illumination

The Illumination area contains the energy of enlightenment, fame and recognition. The PUBLIC RELATIONS or MARKETING department would be best suited here.

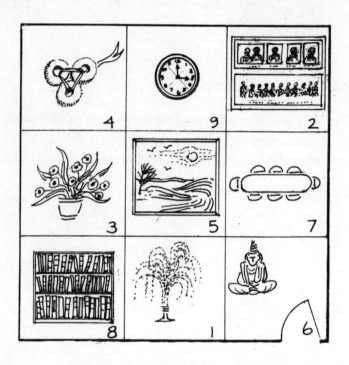

OFFICE PLACEMENT GUIDE & THE BAGUA

PLACEMENT GUIDE FOR
THE OFFICE & THE BAGUA

Area No 1—Journey

Water features—such as fish tanks, seascapes, fountains representing progression.

Area No 2—Relationships

Pictures of office outings—such as Christmas parties or staff cricket teams to represent relationships with clients and colleagues.

Area No 3—Elders

Pictures of sunrises, fresh flowers in a vase or large plants to represent your advisers.

Area No 4—Fortunate Blessings

Money tree plants, water features, three gold coins tied with a red ribbon, or a small treasure chest to represent luck and prosperity.

Area No 5—Unity

Healthy landscapes or a large ceramic sculpture to enhance stability as this space represents the health of your enterprise.

Area No 6—Helpful Friends

Pictures or sculptures of your spiritual idols such as a Buddha to represent guidance and source of inspiration.

Area No 7—Creativity

Conference areas and project desks to represent your future. A crystal vase to energise the space with vibrant rainbow colours.

Area No 8—Wisdom

Computers, heavy books, files, bookshelves and reference material to symbolise knowledge and contemplation

Area No 9—Illumination

Awards, certificates, presents, trophies, and paintings with predominantly red colours to represent recognition and reputation.

DESK PLACEMENT GUIDE & THE BAGUA

PLACEMENT GUIDE FOR THE DESK & THE BAGUA

Journey: (Middle bottom) You are sitting in this space

Relationships: (Far right) Telephone/ Mobile or any instrument of communication.

Elders: (Middle left) This is the past. Your incoming post tray.

Fortunate Blessings: (Far left) A small potted plant, a small wooden sculpture of your favourite deity, some coins in a box and, possibly, your computer.

...ity: (Middle) This is your work area. Keep it clean, ...dy and free of clutter.

Helpful Friends: (Near right) Calculator, paper clips, a small stapler, colourful pens, pencils, etc.

Creativity: (Middle right) This is your future. Your outgoing mail tray.

Wisdom: (Near left) Reference material, files, books, etc.

Illumination: (Middle top) Red objects like paperweights, a red desk clock, a small trophy.

GLOSSARY

Aura Energy field outside all living bodies.

Bagua Octagonal grid used for locating the various sectors of your life in your office.

Celestial Belonging to heaven or divine.

Ch'i Cosmic energy force, which exists in the environment, underground and within us.

Clutter Things which you possess but neither use nor love.

Cutting Ch'i Inauspicious energy line emanating from a sharp, pointed object or structure (also known as poison arrow).

121

Dowsing A procedure to detect negative earth energy and EMF with the use of instruments like rods or pendulums.

EMF Electromagnetic Field.

Feng Shui (pronounced *Fung Shwa*y) means wind and water. It is the art of balancing the environment and living in harmony.

Five elements Water, wood, fire, soil and metal.

Geopathic stress The effect of negative earth energies, detrimental to your well-being.

Harmony Bliss.

Poison Arrow See cutting Ch'i.

122

Relationship

corner Far right area of your office from the front door corresponding to your clients and colleagues.

Wealth

corner Far left area of your office from the front door corresponding to prosperity and wealth.

Yin and

Yang Two opposite and complementary types of cosmic energy forces. Yin is dark, passive and receptive energy. Yang is light, positive and creative energy.

Happiness is not a state to arrive at, but a manner of travelling.

Accentuate the positive, eliminate the negative.

Happiness does not depend upon who you are or what you have, it depends solely upon what you think.

Life just is. You have to flow with it. Give yourself to the moment. Let it happen.

Thoughts are energy. And you can make your world or break your world by your thinking.

Peace is the fairest form of happiness.

The goal of life is living in agreement with nature.